East Anglian Cottages

By

J. M. Proctor

With Illustrations and Photographs by the Author

PROVIDENCE PRESS

First published August 1979

Reprinted with minor ammendments April 1981

TO MOLLY

Published by Providence Press, Wardy Hill, Ely, Cambridgeshire

ISBN 0-903803-05-4

Printed by Hobbs, King & Parr, Soham, Ely, Cambs.

CONTENTS

ACKNOWLEDGEMENTS

My thanks are to very many people indeed. To my wife for recording observations to ensure that I drove safely and for typing the text. Also to many cottagers and bricklayers, colleagues (especially H.J. Mason) and libraries.

But how can I express my gratitude to those who have given me the pleasures I have written of here, those who have maintained their homes and buildings in their local character which I trust will be increasingly appreciated as the years go by.

J.M.P.

FOREWORD

In this book I have set out to record the wide and delightful variety of building styles and materials to be found in East Anglia.

Here is a new way of viewing the countryside — to give extra interest to any visit within the area or simply a pleasant pastime for tedious car journeys — at least for the passengers! Hopefully East Anglians may find in it a little that is new.

It is nearly thirty years since I began collecting the records on which this book is based, and although not every narrow lane has been travelled nor all villages studied in equal detail this is by no means a sketchy picture. Necessarily many of the earlier records needed to be re-assessed as old buildings are so readily lost or modified. Indeed I hope very much that readers will be kind enough to tell me of any inaccuracies in text and maps and possibly even supply additional information.

The attempt has been made to restrict records to seemingly 'native' architecture. Thus I have excluded most of the larger country houses where the style is clearly of a national flavour where, no doubt, the architect was a man of high reputation whose aim was to build to current fashion with a main eye to enhancing his own reputation amongst all the upper classes, not just the local gentry. Likewise excluded are the 'follies' of the rich, the cottage groups built to a style which the Lord of the Manor fancied but derived little or nothing from the contemporary buildings in the neighbourhood.

Some apology must be made for the title of this book. For it to be truly accurate it would have been far too long! Certainly for the most part it is about cottages — small dwellings of the working classes. But all buildings, other than Churches and those just mentioned, have been considered, especially outbuildings, which tend to receive less attention from the restorer and moderniser than do houses, and therefore may better reflect the character of the area.

Usually outbuildings are very similar in construction to their contemporary houses. In some places they necessarily differ; thus cattle are most unlikely to treat wattle and daub with sufficient care and attention! So south of the main flint belt we can find that while the houses are largely wattle and daub, the outbuildings are of weather-boarding and boundary walls of flint. Many of our best illustrations will be seen to be of outbuildings.

Finally I hope this book will stimulate the traveller to see more of interest in cottage styles elsewhere in the country. Hopefully he will not be too disappointed, since nowhere compares in variety and distinctness of styles with East Anglia. Nevertheless it can be fascinating, for example, to contrast the erectness of the thatch of the Suffolk roof with the Hampshire Cottage where windows and doors seem to peep out from what almost seems to be a thatch blanket attempting to cover everything. The industrial Midlands have lost almost all of their true cottage heritage but there the diligent may find delight in the need to hunt even more carefully for district characteristics.

29 Park Lane   J. M. PROCTOR
Histon, Cambridge   JANUARY 1979

INTRODUCTION

Pattern of East Anglia

Time mellowed cottages, crumbling with age and from neglect are so easily bulldozed to oblivion. The spaces where they stood, perhaps for centuries, are, in a short time filled by a new set of houses looking just the same as so many others in the village and indeed throughout the country. The monotonous design of our modern homes of near functional perfection adds nothing to the charm of the village. It takes so long for them to soften amidst their newly planted shrubs and trees, and only when they do will the neighbourliness, the soul of sound society, of the original village be regained.

Eye pleasing weathered and lichen tinted tiles, poor fitting, letting in a little cold and rain, are crushed to hardcore and replaced by machine perfected, standardized designs. Can they inspire a painting from a child across the street? — they are too commonplace.

Small-framed windows disappear long before their time to give way to larger frames and larger panes, which let in more light but let out more heat. It is sad that the new are of such national uniformity when there is little economic need for it. Environmental regimentation gathers speed and we fly to more and more exotic holidays to try to escape it all.

Made of the land on which they stand

Tune your eyes to screen out such monotony and the older world of character and charm will reappear. Then you will delight in what remains of the cottages and smaller houses of long past generations with their wonderful variety in style and in the materials from which they were contrived. Far more variety exists in East Anglia than in any other part of the country of comparable size.

The ill-fed, ill-clad labourer of scythe and sickle days built — of straight necessity — with what lay closest to his parents' doors. High energy consuming, leisured modern man can hardly comprehend his situation. Even those who prospered — mainly tradesmen — built but a little better. Choice of materials was stringently restricted by the transport cost. Picture the slowly plodding horse and cart with tiny load; the roads rough, sometimes near impassible with mud, and the pace good at some 20 miles a day. Cheaper to flaunt one's little wealth by decorative use of local materials, than send for loads of 'foreign' goods on journeys taking many days.

Thus each village basically reflects the local geology. Add to the wood and stone which lay around, the subtleties and quirks of craftsmanship developed over centuries in comparatively isolated communities and in spite of the harsh limitations imposed by their circumstances, it is remarkable what variations of form could be achieved, few displeasing to the eye, many artistically unrivalled.

With present day materials and construction techniques we can build our homes to almost any shape. Those living in close view of some modern contrivances deserve our sympathy — perhaps a rate rebate!

This booklet attempts to record a little of this fading pattern of the past. No great degree of accuracy is now possible. Time has destroyed the weakest — thatch oft replaced by tile, timber by brick or stone. The village we see now perhaps is all the more attractive for the loss of its meanest dwellings, hovels of the poorest of the poor, the sick, the aged; but who knows they might have added even greater interest to the scene.

Look at a wall

It is perhaps surprising what a wide range of materials can be employed to make a good house wall. The essential feature is that the corners are of regular shape and adequate strength. Bricks or ashlar (i.e. carved smooth and rectangular) stone, neatly overlapping each other, clearly provide the best stability. But the flattish, rough, limestone pieces used for drystone walling of the field make good house walls when skilfully used with shaped stone for corners. Flints on the other hand, have little natural stability but when set in mortar can stand up to a thousand years or more. Flint houses with brick 'dressing' (i.e. lintels, cills and wall corners) which often stand on brick footings, need a good roof to keep rain from the mortar which might otherwise soften allowing the wall to crumble.

Mud walls require even more protection overhead and at their feet than flint. A Devonshire saying is that 'All cob (mud walling) wants is a good hat and a good pair of shoes'.

What could be cheaper than spreading mud from a hole in the garden, over interwoven spars or thin branches cut from close-by wood or hedgerow. Such 'wattle and daub' is thus little more expensive than the timber frame needed to hold it. In much of Suffolk, Essex and Cambridgeshire such walling is very common, and often the surface is decorated with simple shallow patterning: rarely, there is ornate decoration of the plaster ('pargetting'), in deep relief, depicting flowers, leaves, fruit, branches and other objects.

Unbaked mud, 'clay lump' bricks were made 'on the premises' using a pit in the garden or close by. They are more versatile and strong than they would seem — given the necessary weather protection above and below. Their presence easily goes unnoticed as corners can be as perfectly 'square' as those of a normal brick house and their plaster covering no different from that frequently used on a modern dwelling. Often they are hidden by a skin of normal bricks. Clay lump bricks of outbuildings are frequently protected by a covering of tar.

Roof meets gable wall

The join of the roof with gable wall presents difficulties both in construction and in weather proofing. However, it has given builders great opportunities for variety and decoration. In its simplest form (Fig 1) the roof tiles extend just to the outer edge of the gable wall and there is no scope for a craftsman's decorative skills. Most commonly the roof extends beyond the gable wall (Fig 2) to give weather protection to the most vulnerable uppermost bricks, stonework or plaster. In this case protection is usually given to the ends of the timbers that carry the tiles by 'barge boards' (Fig 4). These were sometimes beautifully decorated but

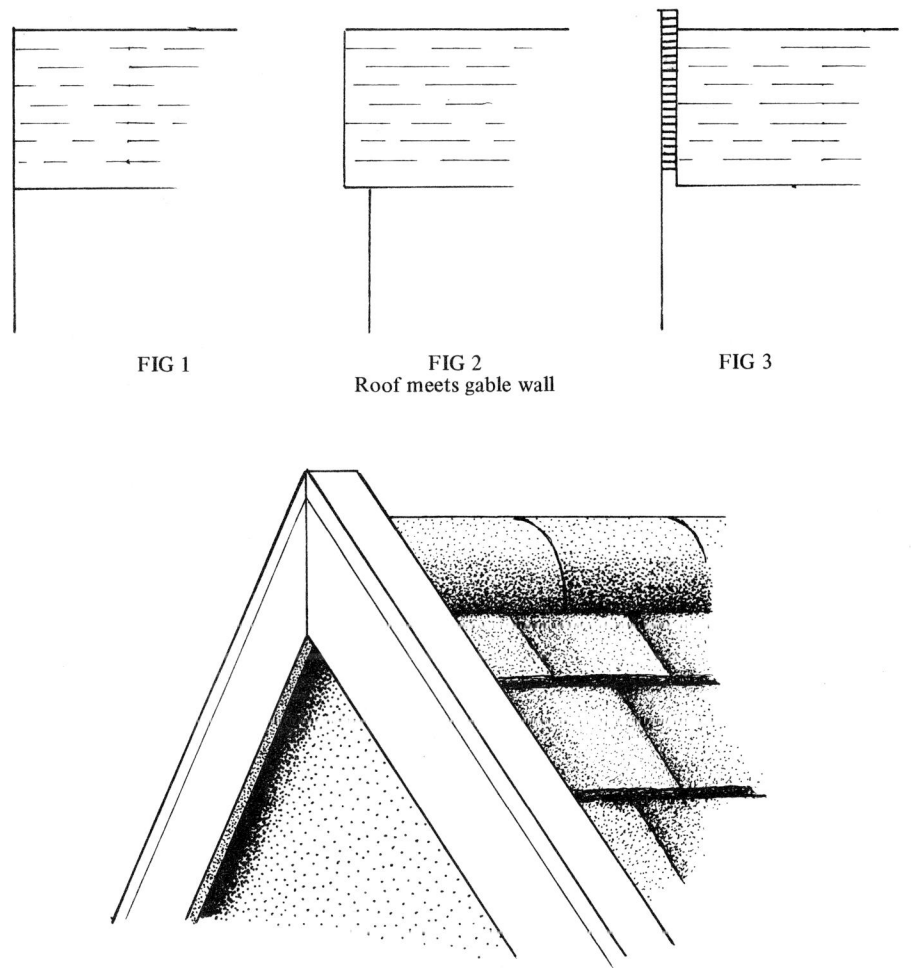

FIG 1   FIG 2   FIG 3
Roof meets gable wall

FIG 4   Simple barge board

specimens of such are rare, for the wood in this position on the house is especially subject to rotting due to wet weather. In the third type (Fig 3) the gable wall extends above the roof level giving protection from strong winds to the tiles or thatch but leaving the top bricks vulnerable to frosting. Often such walls are capped by tiles or 'bricks' of special strength and shape. There are several common ways of setting plain bricks in this 'protecting' position. (Fig. 5). Such wall and roof arrangement includes the particularly attractive 'Dutch' (Fig 16) and Crow stepped gables.

FIG 5   Variations in the setting of bricks on top of gable walls, with an example (left) of 'tumbling' in.

Chimney in a wall

Add a chimney to the gable wall (what a waste of heat!) and you soon realize that there are very many ways in which it can be done. The chimney may lie flush with the wall, be right outside the wall, and in some parts of the country it is, just occasionally, found detached from the house just above the level of the hearth, while often it is half-in and half-outside the wall. Chimney profiles vary greatly. Some of them have a clearly defined distribution as instanced by the Suffolk chimney (Fig 26 and Map 2). Usually the chimney is of the same material as the wall but obviously not so in timber dwellings. Sometimes it is of brick in a flint or limestone wall but often where the gable wall is of these materials the chimney above the roof line is continued in brick. In limestone houses the chimney above the roof line is frequently of the stone itself, never so with flint.

Windows in the roof

Loft extensions have become a popular way of adding another room or two to the modern house. One wonders how many of the dormer windows in old dwellings are the result of the same pressure for room space, though many seem to have been built as part of the basic house design with a sound sense of space economy. Dormer windows vary greatly in design, some types being more common in one area than another.

The simple wedge dormers (Fig 6), most usually found in pantile roofs, would seem by far the easiest to construct, especially those which run from ridge to eaves.

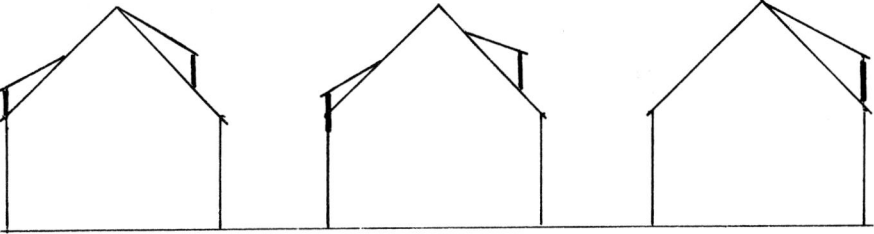

FIG 6   Simple wedge dormers

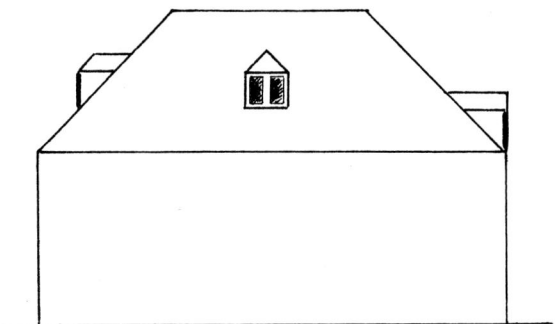

FIG 7   Ridged roofed dormers

FIG 8   Flat or nearly flat roofed dormers

11

The most common dormer has its own simple ridged roof (Fig 7, centre and right) but may lie at different levels in the roof, as do the hipped dormers (Fig 7 left) which occur more frequently in the grander houses; their shape blending nicely with the roof slope. Flat or nearly flat roofed dormers (Fig 8), seem most common in 'town' houses and more nearly approach our present loft extensions in their shape although more graceful due to their smaller size.

In thatch roofs the dormers are often little more than a gentle lifting of the thatch whose depths gives scope for this. The base of the window may well be at the floor level of the room, or very little above it. The semicircular dormer in the centre of the drawing (Fig 9) occurs both in thatch and tile roofs only near Ampthill in Bedfordshire, the dormer on the left is the one most commonly found in thatch; that on the right occurs mostly in Suffolk but is not common. Often tiled dormers, of various shapes can be found rather awkwardly inserted into thatch roofs.

FIG 9   A variety of dormer shapes in thatch with Suffolk gable peak, and typical pattern in shallow relief decoration.

FIG 10 Mansard shaped roof giving more space in the 'loft'. The window — which slides open horizontally — is common in some areas. The drip board helps to throw rain off the plaster wall.

Windows

Windows open in three main ways, the commonest being the casement or side-hinged window. Sash windows are very common too, particularly in larger or relatively modern houses. The horizontal sliding window (Fig 10) tends to be small; this is common in Huntingdonshire but can be found almost anywhere. A few distinctly local types of casement windows exist, there being a notable one in parts of Suffolk. (Fig. 27 & Map 5).

Bricks

Bricks are particularly fascinating in their variation of colour, size and bonding. Red bricks are to be found almost everywhere, but pink, yellow, white and other coloured varieties can be found in differing areas. The distribution of several types are shown on the maps.

Roof

The thatch of earliest dwellings — reed, rushes and other grasses so readily available from marsh and ditch — has slowly been replaced by tiles — and it is surprising that so much remains.

Clay roofing tiles with all their variety, are considered in detail later in this book. Attractive stone tiles ('Collyweston slates') dominate our limestone area. (Map 6)

13

1 MATERIAL FOR WALLS

FLINT

Almost any land can be used for the grazing of animals but stones can make arable farming very difficult and sometimes impossible. To bring most soil into cultivation it was therefore necessary to remove at least the largest stones. Fortunately very good uses could be found for them. They were invaluable for making roads more passable in wet places and for their general improvement almost everywhere. Most stones could also be used as building material, at least when employed in conjunction with brick or 'quality' stone for dressing corners, windows, and door frames.

Pantiled coastal cottages with walls of round wave-worn pebbles built in horizontal courses with red brick to form the corners, and door and window framing. (Holt, Norfolk)

Many areas were fortunate to have stones which did not need mortar and bricks for support. They could readily be used for field boundary walls, often, one imagines, just to find a place to get rid of them, for fields seem to be smallest where stones are most plentiful. Witness the tiny fields in the granite littered areas near Lands End.

While large stones make cultivation impossible, even small ones cause great wear and tear to cultivating equipment and may seriously damage harvesting machines and some crops in the process. Flints are particularly hard and abrasive. In the days before the development of sophisticated hardened steels such wear and tear must have been a very serious matter indeed to the farmers concerned.

Stones work their way to the surface as cultivations proceed so the need for their removal is almost continuous. The author remembers 'picking stones' himself but this is now uneconomic. Interestingly, in the past few years we have seen the development of machines to do the job on a commercial scale.

So expansion of the area of cultivated land, to feed an increasing population, provided a ready supply of materials for cottage building. In the lightly wooded areas such as the chalk lands, this would have been particularly valuable. Indeed hardly any wooden buildings have survived there, in contrast with the common wooden framed buildings of the clay lands of Suffolk, Essex and Cambridgeshire.

FIG 11   Walling of irregular shaped flints, strengthened by brick corners and an occasional brick built through.

Most unbroken flint 'nodules' are silvery white, contrasting very attractively with the red brick which is most usually employed for corners, doors and window framing. Some are very white, others pale brown. The colour much depends on what has happened to the flints after leaving their parent chalk, for the original white coat can absorb some other compounds. In normal atmospheric conditions they will tend to go a little grey, while from lying for a time in certain soils they will take up iron oxides which colour them brown.

In a few villages some extremely large flints have been used; these come from a particular layer in the chalk and are usually broken to make them a more suitable shape for buildings. In fact flint walls usually have a proportion of partly broken 'nodules' so displaying some of the black interior of the flint.

Near the coast flint pebbles from the beaches have been widely used. These — in stark contrast with the knobbly flints from the field and quarry — have been pounded smooth by wave action which has produced a rather different surface,

Brick
chimney
in flint house

sometimes having a tinge of blue. This is because the white coat has been ground off and the exposed dark grey centre of the flint so hammered that the surface is covered with tiny light reflecting fractures.

In later times there was a large usage of flints purposely broken or 'knapped' to display their shining 'black' interior colouring. Such broken surfaces have a peculiar light reflecting character arising from the uniquely curved 'concoidal fractures'. The finest architectural achievement of flint lies without doubt in the 'flushwork' of many churches. This consists of knapped flint pieces shaped to fit into limestone patterns. The visual contrast of the near black and lively reflecting surfaces on matt white backgrounds can be strikingly attractive.

Brick patterns in flint walls are common, – more rare to find a building date. This house also shows how it has been extended, by adding extra height to the existing wall.

Flint back in favour

It is delightful to see that the use of flint is again on the increase. Most frequently it is employed decoratively. The knapped form is least employed due to its high cost, but concrete panels set with flint pebbles or chippings can be found in many recent town centre developments. Such pebbles are also employed as path decoration, almost as they were used in old cobbled roads. Increasingly too, flint walling is being repaired rather than torn down and replaced by wood or brick. Occasionally new flint and red brick buildings are appearing which fit reasonably well into the setting of the old cottages.

History and Prehistory

Chemically, flint is the same as quartz and most sands. It is used in pottery manufacture and, as gravel, is the basis of our modern concrete world.

Geologically it is found only in chalk though the nature of its formation there is still not fully understood. It is particularly hard and its broken edges, being very sharp, made it the most valuable stone for the many thousands of years of the Stone Age. Later it was needed for that very important, but near forgotten, implement, the Strike-a-light.

The 'knapping' of flint was a major industry in the Brandon area of Suffolk. A big steady supply of specially 'cut' flint was required during the 'flintlock gun' era. In that area there is the greatest concentration of flint buildings.

Glacial boulders

Occasionally small brown glacial boulders can be found in the flint walls, having been picked off the land with the flints. It is surprising that these have been so little used in house building but many clay land churches of Cambridgeshire are built almost entirely of them. They may be recognised by their (usually) brown colour and their well rounded shape which has occasional small flat surfaces resulting from their having moved, without rolling, for some distance over abrasive rocks at the base of the glacier. In some churches they form particularly beautiful walls due to the subtle variety of shades of browns, reds and greens. In the sunshine, the south wall of Impington (Cambs) Church is notably attractive.

Decorative flint flushwork — (Long Melford Church, Suffolk)

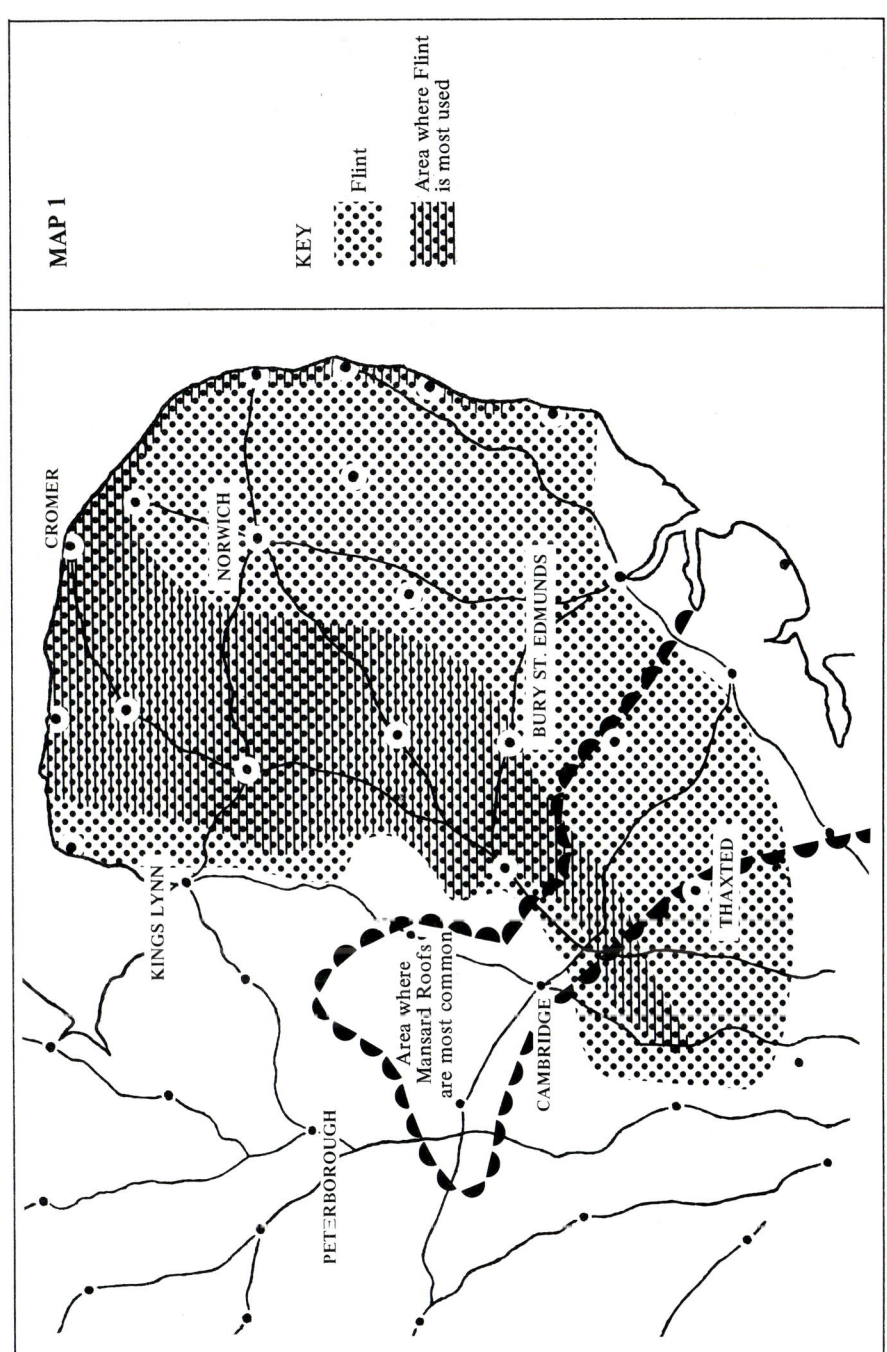

MAP 1

KEY

Flint

Area where Flint
is most used

CROMER

NORWICH

BURY ST. EDMUNDS

THAXTED

KINGS LYNN

Area where
Mansard Roofs
are most common

CAMBRIDGE

PETERBOROUGH

CLAY LUMP

Nowadays when labour costs seem to be the major element in producing practically everything it is difficult to imagine the times when labour was cheap and materials relatively costly. However, the unburnt 'clay lump' brick cost almost nothing apart from time, for they were made with the very cheapest of ingredients — mud reinforced with straw. The only real cost was the wear and tear on the wooden moulds.

The mud was thoroughly puddled with the straw and pressed firmly into moulds; then the moulds were removed and the bricks left to dry before being used. In drying they were likely to shrink a little, which was one reason for not using them immediately. The puddling destroyed, at least temporarily, the natural lines of fracturing in the 'clay' and so reduced its proneness to break-up by weathering.

What made a suitable clay? Clearly anything with much humus in it, such as most top-soil could not be used as it would be too liable to fall to pieces in a short time, for the value of humus in a soil is that it helps to break it up to make a good tilth. Likewise clays which break up readily under frost action would be unsuitable and very sandy soil would crumble too easily. Certainly the distribution map of clay lump (Map 2) suggests that it was not used to any extent on the heaviest clay

Clay lump outhouse — a well built structure but with its protective skin of tarred plaster crumbling away. (Long Stratton, Norfolk)

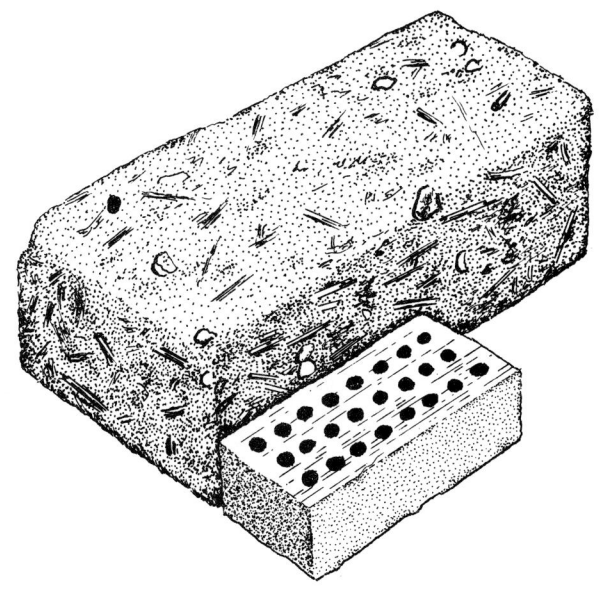

FIG 12 'Clay lump' brick showing comparison with brick of normal size.

lands where good brick clay was plentiful nor on the sandiest areas and the fens. It is also absent in the limestone area simply because so much better building material was readily available.

How far did the clay lump makers know what material was really suitable to use?

Analysis of clay lump from three villages gave the following percentage figures of their different particle sizes.

Villages	Clay	Intermediates	Sand	Pebbles	Chalk
Melbourne	5	4	4	Nil	87
Wixoe	16	18	23	Nil	43
Landbeach	17	20	53	10	Nil

The differences between these three are considerable — from nearly pure chalk to quite a sandy material — and show how very wide a range of subsoil was used; hardly any one of them approaches a material suitable for making baked bricks. In colour they range from pale browns to off-white in the chalky areas of South Cambridgeshire. Their size is usually about 18 ins x 8 ins x 6 inches, but larger sizes can be found.

FIG 13 'Clay lump' boundary walling protected from rain by clay tiles, and from rising damp by brick footing.

FIG 14 'Clay lump' house in process of demolition showing how even chimneys could be made of this apparently unstable material.

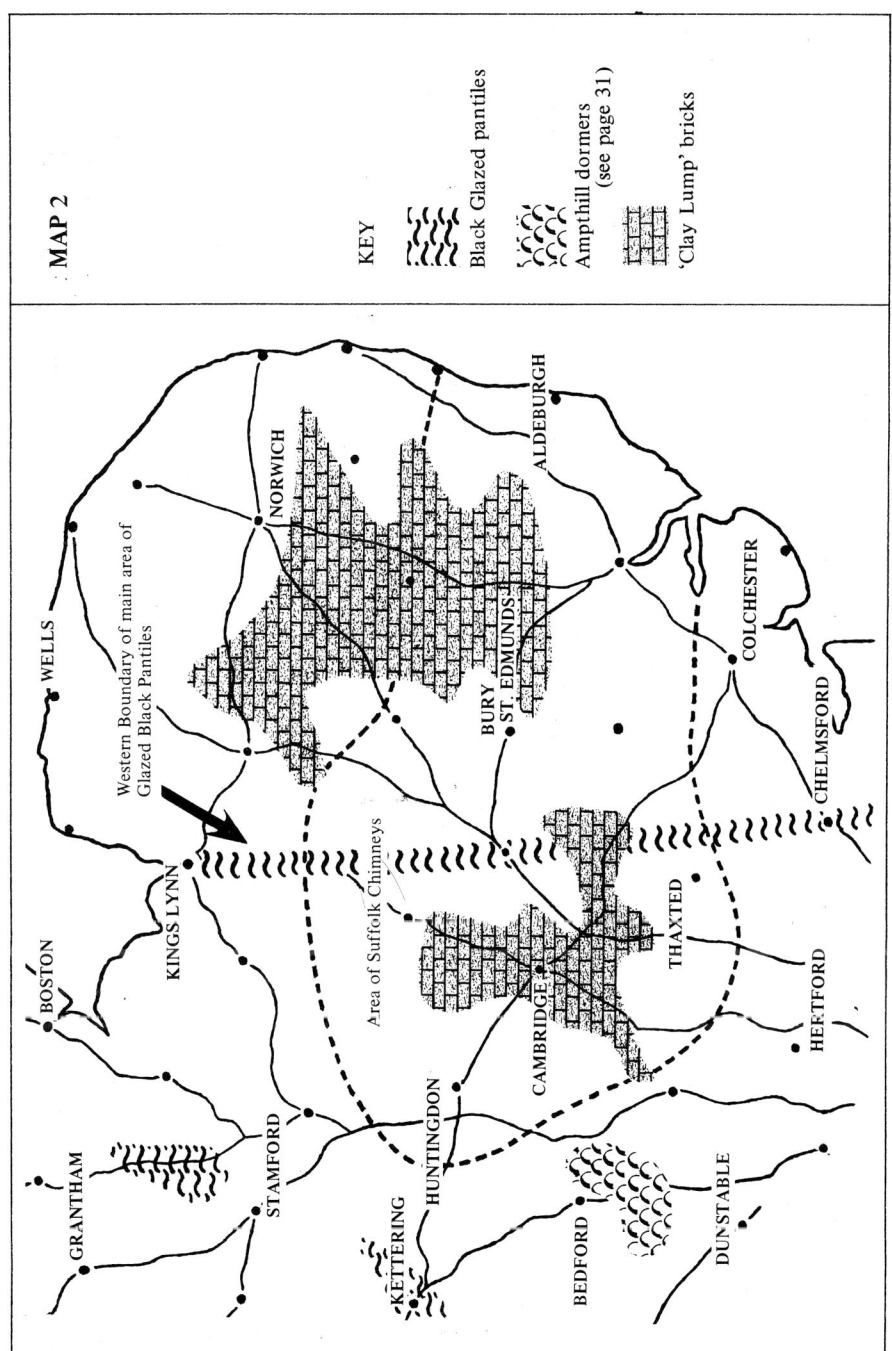

MAP 2

KEY

~~~ Black Glazed pantiles

∽∽∽ Ampthill dormers
(see page 31)

▦ 'Clay Lump' bricks

WELLS

BOSTON

GRANTHAM

STAMFORD

KETTERING

HUNTINGDON

BEDFORD

DUNSTABLE

HERTFORD

CHELMSFORD

COLCHESTER

ALDEBURGH

NORWICH

KINGS LYNN

CAMBRIDGE

THAXTED

BURY
ST. EDMUNDS

Western Boundary of main area of
Glazed Black Pantiles

Area of Suffolk Chimneys

23

CLUNCH

Everyone is familiar with the soft white chalk which covers, like a thick blanket, so much of the south and east of England. Less familiar are the several thin layers of very hard chalk which lie within this blanket. This stone is usually known as 'clunch', although geologically designated as Totternhoe Stone, Melbourn Rock and Chalk Rock. It has been widely used in both house and church building and for road foundation. (Map 3)

Compared with the limestone of the north-west of our area, clunch is very soft and rather subject to frost damage. With increasing prosperity it has therefore been replaced by the 'Stamford' limestones for churches (notably in Cambridge) and by brick for houses. However, due to the ease with which it can be carved, it has been used to produce some of the most beautiful and delicate stonecarving in the country, as can be seen particularly well in the Lady and Chantry Chapels of Ely Cathedral.

The best clunch walling can be found in a few villages south of Cambridge where each stone is so accurately shaped that the mortar is very thin. Almost half of clunch walling is of 'rubble' pieces.

FIG 15 Clunch wall strengthened with brick corners. In the area just south of Cambridge the clunch was cut to particularly regular shapes with a good smooth face. Note thin mortar between blocks, and effects of weathering.   Severe cracking at top is due to a leaking roof.

MAP 3

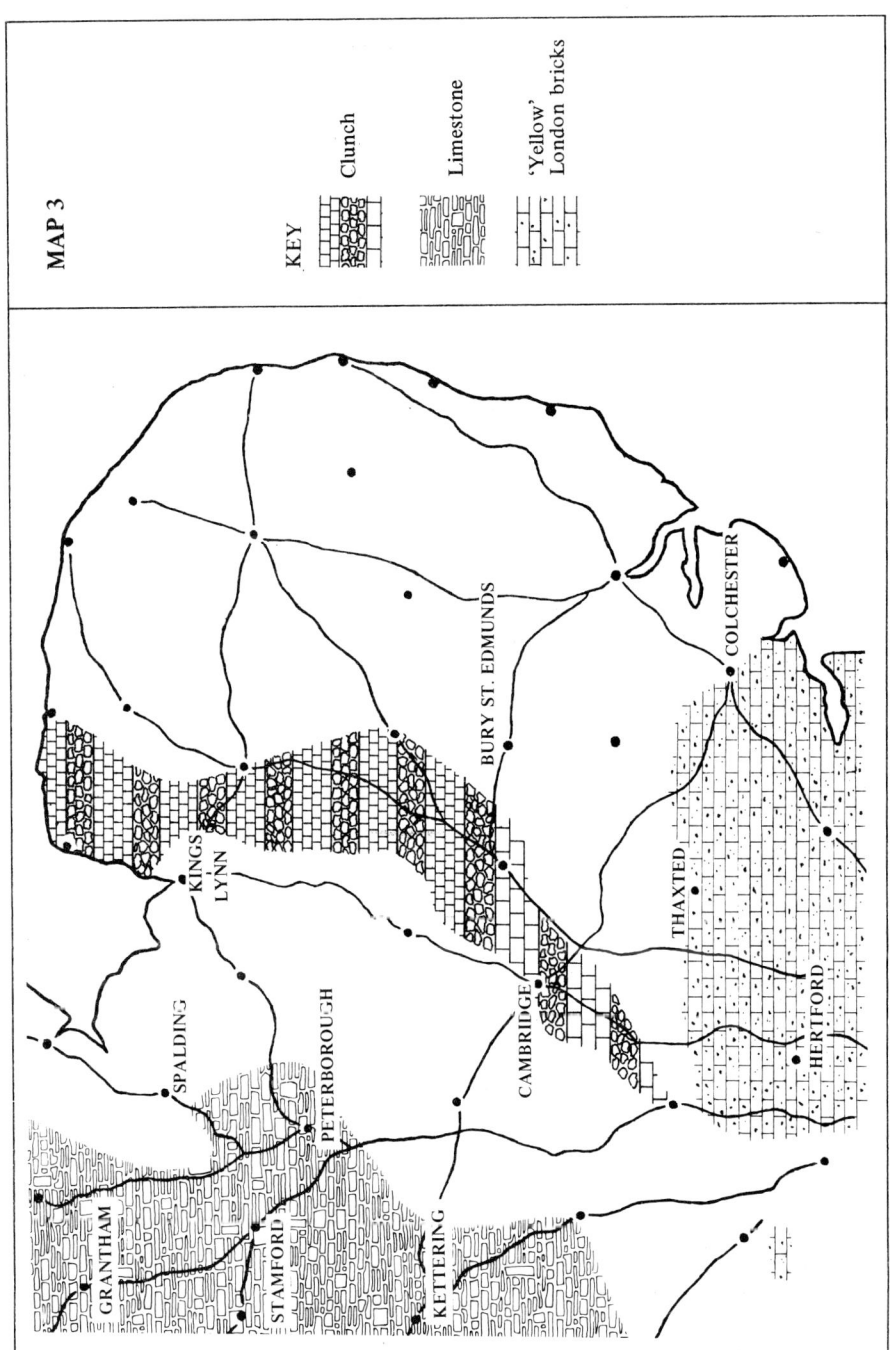

KEY

Clunch

Limestone

'Yellow'
London bricks

COLCHESTER

BURY ST. EDMUNDS

KINGS
LYNN

THAXTED

SPALDING

HERTFORD

PETERBOROUGH

CAMBRIDGE

GRANTHAM

STAMFORD

KETTERING

BRICKS – THE POOR RELATION

Perhaps the biggest impact of modern art on the general public in recent years was the appearance of a pile of bricks at the Tate Gallery. Not surprisingly, reaction was somewhat hostile. We have not been brought up to see anything beautiful in bricks, they are too commonplace.

But stop for a while and look closely at old bricks in a good warm sunlight and see how they glow with colour. In this over-mechanized age most of us find something oddly pleasing about anything worked by hand. Perhaps it is the minor 'imperfections', the subtle variations in colour, shape and surface texture which give old bricks some special lively quality of their own.

Colour of bricks depends mainly on the chemical content of the clay. The red colour arises from the effect of high temperature on an iron compound; a certain proportion of chalk in the clay ensures a non-red brick. The degree of heat also effects the colour; the 'blue' ends (headers) of some bricks are due to their receiving greater heat through the manner the bricks were stacked in the kiln.

In the eighteenth century 'common' red brick became treated with disdain in certain fashionable quarters, and pale grey bricks were produced to give more of a stone-like appearance. Quite often, whatever was the locally more fashionable brick or stone, was used for the front wall only.

Crinkle crankle wall. Its sinuous shape makes it self strengthening – very frequent massive buttressing would otherwise be needed. (Easton, Woodbridge, Suffolk.)

Beginning with the Romans

Bricks were produced in quantity in Roman times as witness the vast numbers subsequently gathered from Verulamium to build St. Alban's Cathedral. Where have all the Roman bricks gone from all the other brick Roman towns? The Roman brick was much thinner than our own, almost a tile and serving slightly different construction purposes.

Brick making began again in England in the twelfth century and this was in East Anglia whose close trade and cultural ties with Europe (besides a lack of good building stone) no doubt gave the necessary impetus.

Use of bricks increased slowly but steadily from that time in parallel with increased prosperity and with consequent improvement in housing standards. A boom in brick making was created by the population explosion which followed the Industrial Revolution. Mechanized production processes began to be used.

During the earlier centuries brick making was a very local business; pockets of suitable clay were fortunately well distributed over East Anglia which has been in the forefront of brick development up to the present time of the massive brick industries near Bedford, and Peterborough. Naturally mass production techniques tended to produce a relatively drab and uniform product, but at very much lower cost than those of the old fashioned small works, which quickly went out of business between the two wars. Since the last war, however, the demand for more visually pleasing 'facing' bricks has steadily increased and there has been a good demand for handmade bricks – although the 'mass industry' has now found ways of making similar looking products with variations in shade, 'wrinkles' and general texture. Cost should no longer preclude the use of a pleasing looking brick – at least on the front wall!

Making bricks

It is not difficult to make bricks – the problem is how to produce them efficiently in terms of labour, fuel and product quality. A great deal of energy is usually required to pound and pummel raw clay – with the right amount of water into a plastic state. For centuries this required hard hand labour, then there were horse driven pugging mills and later steam was employed. Stones and other impurities had to be removed; sometimes a proportion of sand was added.

Moulding the individual bricks defied mechanisation longest. From the moulds the 'green' hand made bricks were taken immediately and carefully stacked to dry under simple coverings for some months varying with the time of year.

Firing was done either in clamps or in permanent kilns. The former were particularly appropriate for on-site manufacture for a special building. The 'green' bricks were stacked together with some of the fuel which would be needed, roughly walled and then sealed over with clay.

The temperature and time needed to fire bricks depends on the type of clay and type of brick required. Something like 1000° centigrade for about two days takes some skill in achieving in a kiln – in a clamp it meant a wide range of quality in the product with a high proportion of 'throw-outs'. Temperature control in kilns was a skill acquired by experience and could be only rough and ready by modern standards. Late improvements in kiln design assisted in achieving more even firing temperature. The building of kilns next to each other (e.g. in a circle) led to much fuel saving as heat from a kiln being fired helped warm up its newly filled neighbour, instead of all the heat of firing being lost to the air. It might take about a week for a kiln to cool enough to be emptied.

Wood, turves and coal were used in firing according to what was available or could be afforded. It could require a ton of coal to make 4,000 bricks with some types of kiln needing coaling every 40 minutes. The big advantage of the Bedford/ Peterborough clay is that it happens to contain most of the fuel required to fire it! The slave labour conditions of brickyard work have fortunately gone, but the hand made brick industry has left us a tremendous heritage — infinitely fascinating.

From the author's collection: a great brick — probably to reduce tax (East Suffolk), a common red brick with building date incised (Over, Cambs.), a pale cream brick with maker's name, indicating his pride in his product.

Qualities of bricks

Bricks have many valuable qualities which are easily overlooked. In the first place is their high resistance to heat, thus making them particularly suitable for chimneys. They were used for this purpose in some stone and flint houses, though this is partly because it is easier to build a chimney of brick, due to their regular size and shape. The increased availability of bricks made the introduction of chimneys into wooden houses more practical, particularly for the poorer classes — a distinct advance over open central hearth and hole in the roof.

The disaster of the Great Fire of London reminds us how unsafe are wood and thatch in town construction. In most parts of the country brick was the only reasonably cheap and safe alternative walling material.

Chimney of unusual design with elaborate but graceful patterning in 'rubbed' (carved) bricks. Note 'crow-stepped' gable. (Methwold, Norfolk)

Cottage of no uncertain date.

A delightful Norfolk cottage of coursed flint with pantiled mansard roof, dormer windows, and gable wall rising above the roof level. The village sign remains but its charming backcloth has been demolished. (Litcham, Norfolk)

Charming cottages of lathe and plaster walling under cosy thatched roofs. Dreamy country dwellings near the industrial town of Haverhill. (Withersfield, Suffolk)

Semicircular dormer windows found only in Ampthill, Beds, and surrounding villages under both thatch and red flat tile roofs. Their timber framed walls are completed with nogging of red brick.

Attractive row of cottages varying delightfully in their design, in Rupert Brooke's Grantchester. They are maintained by the Cambridgeshire Cottage Improvement Society.

Bricks also can provide good heat insulation — as long as they are dry — as they are full of tiny 'bubbles' of air. Pockets of clay suitable for brick making could be found not too far distant from most East Anglian villages, many of which had their own permanent brick works. Thus the cost of transport was not excessive and the bricks relatively cheap in consequence.

Bricks are remarkably inert in so much as lichens and mosses do not grow on them — unlike nearly all types of stone. Brick is also not decayed by the atmospheric contaminants such as sulphur which so affects limestone — even granite is more readily weathered. Frost splitting is the only hazard and this usually applies only to bricks whose top surfaces are exposed to rain; a few types of brick tend to become frost weathered at the base of the wall, especially in the absence of a damp proof course.

While bricks can be made to practically any size and shape the dimensions to which they have gradually become standardised are based on two simple criteria. Firstly they are a weight and size which well fits the hands of the bricklayer. Secondly each brick has good strength in itself and they are readily bonded (fitted) together to give a stable wall — even without mortar they would stand well.

It is surprising how decorative ordinary bricks can be. This may be achieved by patterns of different colours or of profile or by different bondings. (Fig 18).

Limestone is used for the front of this house and less expensive brick for the remainder. (Doddington, Cambs.)

Paler bricks selected to highlight the 'tumbling-in' on a mansard roofed house. (Haddenham, Cambs.)

Decoratively shaped bricks have been produced in considerable quantities. A much better artistic effect is always achieved however — at much higher price — by carving or 'rubbing' bricks to shape — often after they have been laid. The most splendid work of this type has been in the embellishment of chimneys (normally only above roof level) of some of the grander houses in East Anglia and elsewhere.

What of the future? The extreme escalation of labour costs has had a big impact on building as little can be done to speed up the hand laying of bricks. Great efforts have therefore been made to find substitute materials and to explore pre-fabrication techniques. Experiment after experiment has so far been a complete failure. There is still no better method of producing an attractive dwelling than with the old fashioned brick!

Dutch Gables

As may be judged from Figure 16, the Dutch Gable may well be considered as one of the highlights of the bricklayers craft — although some include a proportion of flints, and stone has been used in other parts of the country. Naturally they were built only by the comparatively rich and are not common. They are found more frequently

FIG 16 Detail of particularly fine Dutch gable at Binham (near Wells, Norfolk) and a selection of shapes from elsewhere.

in Norfolk, Suffolk, Cambridgeshire and Lincolnshire than elsewhere. Obviously their origins lie in the close trade and cultural contacts between the Low Countries and Eastern England in earlier times. A few 'crow-stepped' gables can also be found in the larger houses but are rare in comparison with their use in Scotland.

Norfolk Cross

The exposed point of brick gables are often protected by bricks specially made for the purpose. In part of Norfolk however, the use of a little cross-like cap of bricks is common. (Fig. 17, Map 6).

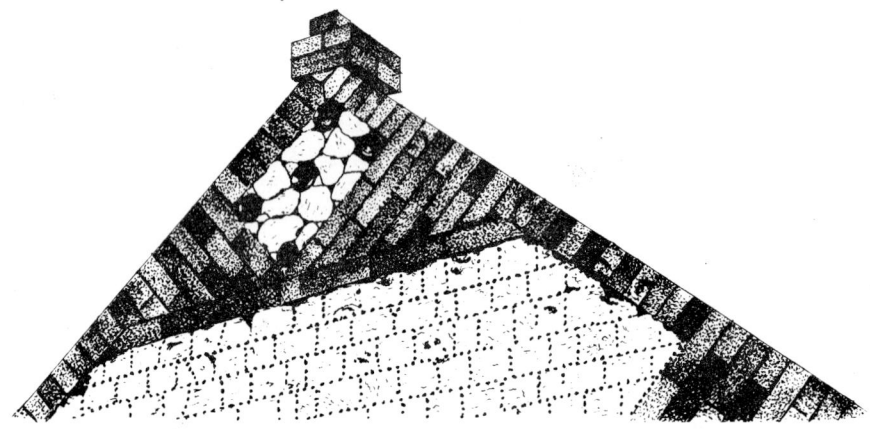

FIG 17   Wall of small clunch bricks with attractive garreting with tiny pieces of carstone (common at Stoke Ferry, Norfolk). Brick cross pattern at ridge is found only in Norfolk. Note bottle bottoms set neatly into the wall.

Brick decoration in a clunch wall. (North Norfolk)

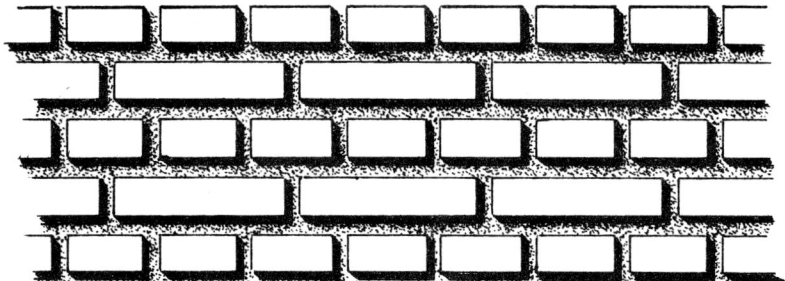

English bond

Stretcher bond — the normal for cavity walls

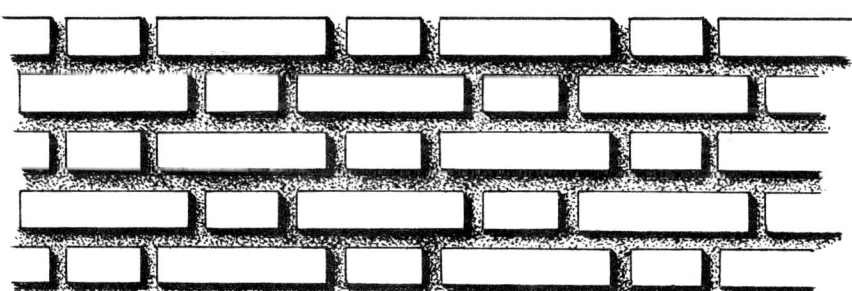

Flemish bond

FIG 18 The most common brick bonds

IRONSTONE

Ironstone occurs in small quantities in quite a number of places where it can sometimes be discovered in church walling. Only in two areas is it available on any scale and so used for domestic architecture; in a belt from Hunstanton to Downham Market and around Corby. (Map 5)

In the former area it occurs in the Lower Greensands from which it has also been taken on a smaller scale in Bedfordshire. It is known as Carstone and is a mid to very dark brown sandstone. There appears to be several 'forms' of the stone although these tend to merge from one to another. In one form the carstone is of thin, sometimes quite tiny, pieces which are set together in almost brick-like fashion, often with mortar not visible from the outside; this is almost always dressed with brick.

Near Hunstanton carstone could be quarried in substantially sized blocks and of this, much of the new town (New Hunstanton) was built around 1870 to 1914. Here, and in buildings of the same period elsewhere in this area much of the stone is ashlar, that is, it can be carved into smooth-faced rectangular blocks. There is a considerable amount of carstone intermediate between the thin layered stone and this 'freestone'. (i.e. stone readily carved into regular shape).

In many older buildings the stone walls are of only roughly rectangular blocks, dark brown and with thick mortar in which tiny pieces of carstone are set. (See garretting below). Some of this stone is a 'puddingstone' or conglomerate.

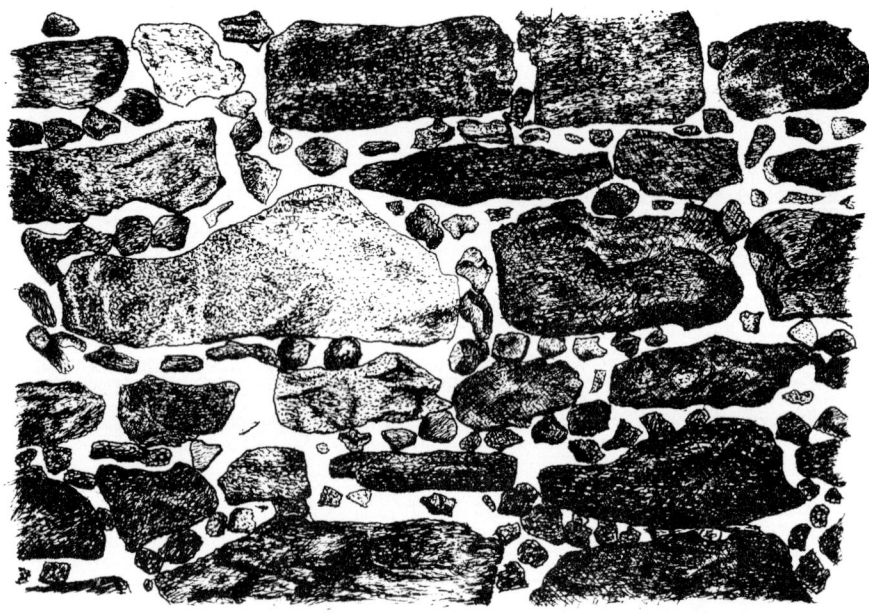

FIG 19 Wall of carstone blocks with garreting of carstone pieces.

There were many carstone quarries and those at Snettisham and Heacham were of considerable size. Besides producing high quality building material these two villages supplied a great deal of stone for stabilizing the navigation channels around the Wash. The industry is still thriving at Snettisham.

Near Downham Market it is thought that most stone, which is largely of the thin variety, was obtained from shallow pits. Its almost prodigal use in that town (e.g. the thick tall boundary walls) suggest a particularly plentiful and readily available source very close, if not within, its boundaries.

Near Corby the ironstone is generally quite pale brown and frequently used in alternating bands with limestone. This stone was the basis of the iron industry in the area.

Bands of pale brown ironstone and limestone found in Gretton and a few other villages near Corby.

Garretting (or Galleting)

The use of small stones around larger ones obviously began as a means of giving extra weather protection to the mortar where there was a gap between the main stones. In some flint walls the garretting of small flint flakes are set so closely together that more than a glance is often necessary to discern their presence. (Map 4)

However, garretting clearly developed from a practical art (Fig 19) into a decorative one with flint or carstone pieces (occasionally small pebbles) used in walls of flint and brick (uncommon), flint alone, carstone and of clunch. Garretting can be found in a few places outside our area in brick-only walls.

Certainly the most striking garretting is where little dark carstone pieces are set in the mortar of ashlar-clunch (Fig 17) as in Stoke Ferry and nearby villages.

Carstone garretting, in the white mortar of walls of the larger, more rectangular carstone, is also very attractive. Flint garretting in flint lacks the contrast needed to give much visual impact and pleasure.

FIG 20   Carstone wall with brick to strengthen corners. The size of the carstone pieces used varies considerably.

FIG 21   Carstone wall with pillar box (Downham Market, Norfolk). The tops of the pillars and wall are covered with tar for protection from the weather.

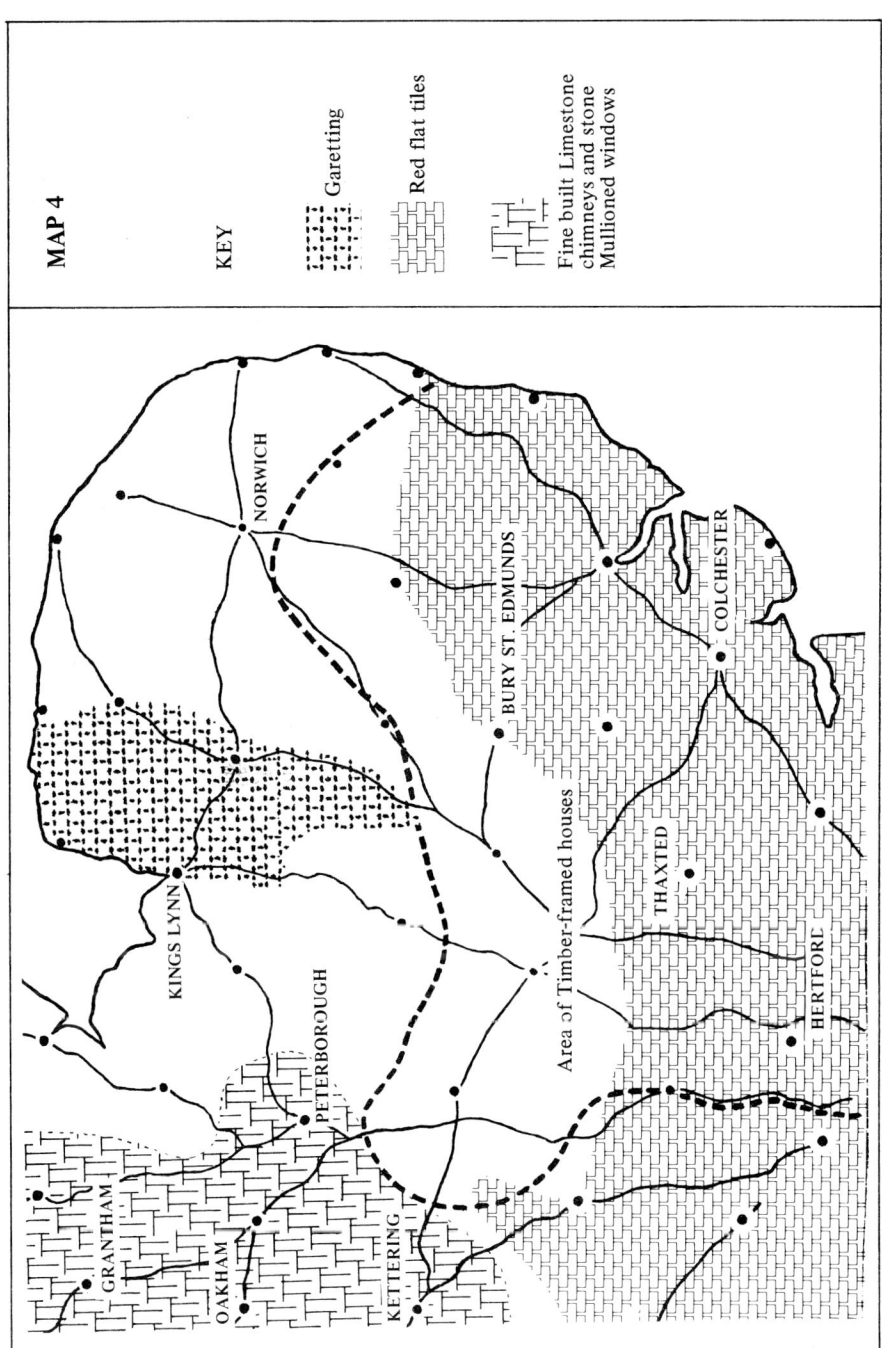

MAP 4

KEY

Garretting

Red flat tiles

Fine built Limestone
chimneys and stone
Mullioned windows

NORWICH

BURY ST. EDMUNDS

COLCHESTER

THAXTED

HERTFORE

Area of Timber-framed houses

KINGS LYNN

PETERBOROUGH

KETTERING

OAKHAM

GRANTHAM

TIMBER

Wood may well be regarded as one of man's very best friends. It is so versatile and so easily shaped to a thousand purposes. It can provide heat, housing of all shapes and sizes, furniture and is an essential part of most simple tools. While the first poor housing must have been little more than interwoven branches covered with mud, even these almost fall into the classifaction of being 'half-timbered' dwellings; though this term tends to be associated in our minds with the rather grander 'black and white' Coaching Inns and houses of Christmas Cards. (Maps 4 & 5)

'Half-timbered' simply means that while all the load bearing members of the building are of strong wood, the spaces between them are filled with other materials. Such infilling was usually of thin branches or spars, covered with mud and straw plaster, these usually being applied outside the timbers, and so hiding them. Sometimes the plaster was replaced later by brick infilling of the timbers; occasionally brick was used at the outset. With many buildings the plaster covering has been removed to display the timbers — where these are of good quality — and this has almost always improved the appearance of the dwelling. Plaster wall covering or 'infilling' is usually known as 'wattle and daub' or 'lath and plaster'; brick infilling of timbers is known as 'nogging'.

'Wattle and Daub' or 'Lath and Plaster' wall

40

An attractive street of half-timbered craftsmens' houses with lath and plaster infilling. (Lavenham, Suffolk)

Pargetting at its finest. (Clare, Suffolk)

In East Anglia the majority of our half-timbered houses are still completely plastered over and so go unrecognised as being basically wood structures. In many cottages the wood is not of such quality as would improve appearances if it could be seen. Nevertheless, we have a great number of buildings where the displayed timbers make a fine sight. Here and there small groups of such houses make particularly pleasant viewing while the small and extremely attractive wool town of Lavenham has extensive rows of timber houses in several adjoining streets — some with overhanging upper floors. Where decoration is added it is usually by way of carvings of parts of the wood framing.

Fires gradually led to the replacement of wooden buildings in towns and, as time went on, the risk of fire reduced its overall use where other materials were readily available; sometimes the local scarcity of wood much encouraged the employment of brick and stone. Wood made it possible to build the wide windows found in Suffolk; lintels are the weakest part of buildings of flint, brick and stone construction.

Brief reference has been made to the decorative relief plasterwork 'pargetting' which is rare, but far rarer elsewhere in this country. Most plaster cottages were decorated with shallow simple patterns 'scratched' into 'panels' of plaster.

The covering of timbers with weatherboarding is rarely attractive but it is common in South Essex. It is said to be the result of the various taxes imposed on bricks from 1784 to 1850 but this seems an unlikely explanation. Weatherboarding

Weatherboarded houses with red flat tiles on roof. (Hunsdon, Herts)

might be more rain repellent than plaster but South Essex is particularly dry — or did wood rot too readily further north? Or were brick taxes imposed more rigorously in the plaster/weatherboard areas than elsewhere? (Map 5). Weatherboarding occurs almost universally in outbuilding constructions. It still really falls into the category of 'half-timbering'; in fact many houses in Essex are part plaster and part weatherboarding. The only 'full-timbered' houses would seem to be the log cabins of last century in North America.

A rare use of decorative weatherboarding. (Hawkedon, Suffolk)

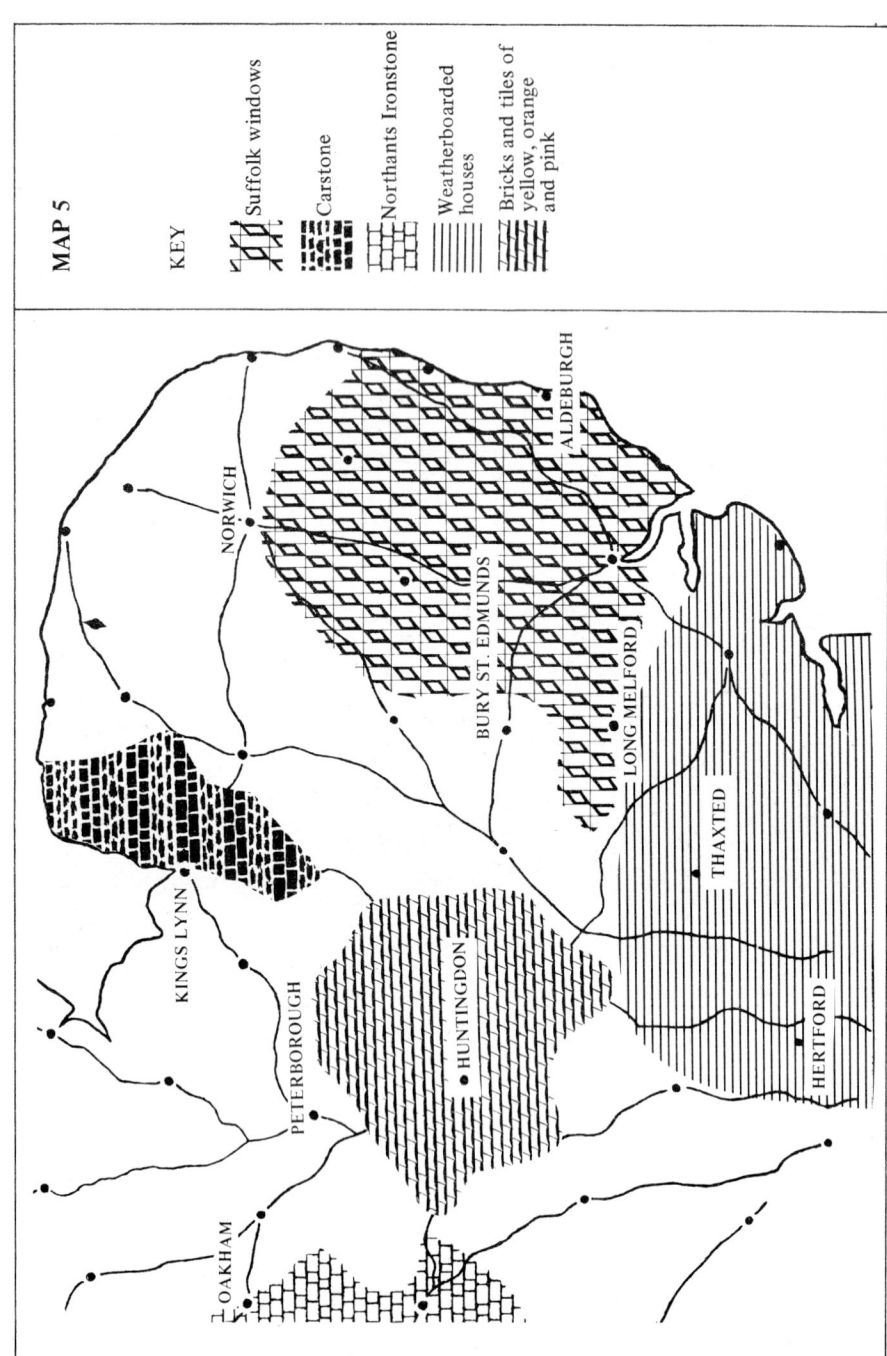

MAP 5

KEY

Suffolk windows

Carstone

Northants Ironstone

Weatherboarded houses

Bricks and tiles of yellow, orange and pink

ALDEBURGH

NORWICH

BURY ST. EDMUNDS

LONG MELFORD

THAXTED

HUNTINGDON

KINGS LYNN

PETERBOROUGH

HERTFORD

OAKHAM

LIMESTONE FOR THE FINEST CRAFTMANSHIP

The north-west of our region may well be regarded as the neglected and unsung northern tip of the Cotswolds, with houses and churches architecturally equal to the more famous parts of Gloucestershire. Many of the limestones of the area are of the finest quality in the country though rather grey than buff-coloured compared with Gloucestershire, and too much soot blackened. The best stone is readily carved, weathers well and is devoid of fractures. That from Barnack was particularly renowned from Roman times until the quarry was exhausted of its 'rag' in the eighteenth century. (Maps 3 & 4)

Transport by water was readily available for the building of castles, monasteries and churches over a wide area. Other notable quarries were at Ketton, Weldon, Ancaster, Clipsham and Kings Cliffe. Several are still producing their high quality material. Large scale maps reveal a profusion of old quarries in the area.

The excellent quality of the stone is well displayed in numerous fine houses (Fig 22); the homes of merchants and more prosperous craftsman. They are built of good, often completely ashlar, stonework, with very clean cut rectangular chimneys topped with a neatly carved bonding course. The windows often have stone mullions and the roofs are always of Collyweston slate.

The numerous beautiful church towers and spires in the neighbourhood also well reflect the quality of the stone and the craftsmen it encouraged.

After a few badly worn stones had been repaired, the black soot was washed from the walls to make Stamford Theatre look as good as new. All that is needed is several million pounds to adequately restore this splendid town and make it a proper inheritance for our children, (Stamford, Lincs.).

FIG 22   One of the most attractive type of houses in the Stamford, Lincs. area. Double-fronted bay windows with stone mullions, Collyweston slate roof, and finely finished stone chimney.

2 MATERIAL FOR ROOFS

CLAY TILES

The roof of a building suffers far greater wear and tear than any other part. Clay tiles are vulnerable to frost, the nails of slate tiles rust and roof timbers rot. Thus there are very few roofs of great age and it is the part of any house to which decorative attention is least given — apart from the case of thatch. Church spires are the only other artistic roof success and are hardly applicable on a wide scale! Many church roofs tend to be purposely hidden by decorative parapets.

The principal roof tile shapes are shown in Figure 24. The pantile is the most universal and tends to be found on smaller houses and on outbuildings. The peculiar hollow tile (Fig 24 right) is very rare and only occurs near Kimbolton.

FIG 23 The universal pantile, hand-made and variable in shape, making a poorly fitting roof. Note slight frosting and spots of lichen on these well weathered tiles.

The general dimensions of each type of tile are fairly standard, (due to Parliamentary directives at various times) but in detail they vary considerably and anyone replacing a few old tiles must take care that they match adequately. The distribution of different tiles is of particular interest, in general being tied more closely to the areas where they were made than is the case with bricks; perhaps because they were likely to suffer much greater damage in transit.

Red pantiles are almost universal but the proportion of them to other tiles varies greatly; north and east of the limestone slates there is little else than red pantiles and red corrugated tiles.

Red flat tiles, absent in the centre of the limestone slate area, appear in the west while in the south they are the most common roofing material (Map 4). They are also not infrequently found on the larger houses in the east of our area.

East of a line from Kings Lynn to Chelmsford black glazed pantiles can be found in almost any village. (Map 2) Their origin is not so far into the past and they belong only to East Anglia. It will be interesting to see (in a few hundred years time!) just how much better weather protection the glaze has given. Glazed tiles are recorded as having been made as early as 1771. In the same area unglazed grey but unattractive pantiles occur here and there.

Particularly attractive, at least when they are clean, are the multicoloured roof tiles (and bricks) around Huntingdon (Map 5). Their true colours seem best described as sunset pastel shades — of yellow, pinks, orange and grey. Sometimes there are several shades — blending one into the other — within a single tile, sometimes the variation is greater between one tile and another, some roofs are predominantly orange, others pale yellow, others pinks. Most are grimy with age but here and there walls have been scrubbed clean and look beautiful. These tiles seem to have been produced from several geological formations of clays but notably from Oxford Clay.

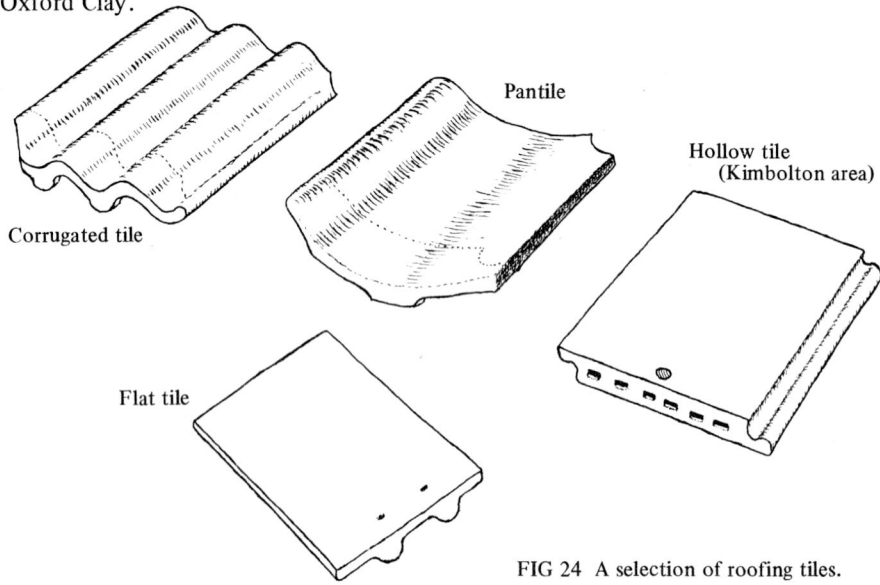

Corrugated tile

Pantile

Hollow tile
(Kimbolton area)

Flat tile

FIG 24 A selection of roofing tiles.

THE MYSTERY OF THATCH

Why do we get so sentimental about thatch? Why too, is it that this most primitive of roofing which, by its nature, needs continuous replacement and repair, has been maintained on such a scale all over the country?

For it is of the very drabbest colour, it is constantly damaged by nesting sparrows and starlings and it has such a high fire risk that it was banned in most towns centuries ago.

The author has no ready explanation, biased as he is by schooldays under slate and holidays under thatch. Admittedly there was, at the back of the mind some slight worry lest the thatch caught fire, even though escape would have been relatively painless from such low-ceilinged buildings. But what a delight each morning to be woken by chirping quarrelling sparrows steadily destroying the thatch within a foot or two of ones head with rustlings in the sloping ceiling even closer.

It could be impossibly hot to get to sleep in town in summer but it never was under that insulating thatch where on a winter evening we were so snugly warm — provided that the draughts which go with a blazing open fire were excluded as best we could.

Bird damage to comparatively new thatch.

It is quite obvious why thatch is the oldest form of roofing. At its simplest it is cheap, for it can be gathered free from ditch and pondside; but obviously some vegetation is much more suitable than others. Straight stems are clearly needed but these must both pack tightly; to throw off the rain, and be as durable as possible. Though possibly more durable, wooden stems cannot be packed tightly enough, so all thatch is of softer annual plant stems.

It is not difficult to get an idea of the relative durability of different vegetation; look for whatever is standing in hedgerow, dyke or marsh after a hard winter and the best survivor is the common reed though there will be other plants as well, rough grasses, rushes, burr-reed and, particularly, giant sedge which with its more flexible leaves is valuable to cover over the top of the ridge.

The common (Norfolk) reed (*Phragmities communis*) is undoubtedly the best thatching material as its stems are long and highly durable, but it is costly due to the labour needed for its harvesting and preparation. In several localities it is cultivated specially for thatching and in the Norfolk Broads, and a few other places, some mechanical harvesting is now practiced. Thatching reed is produced in the National Trust's Wicken Fen in Cambridgeshire.

Re-thatching a barn with Norfolk reeds

Reed is common enough in most parts of the country in ponds and dykesides and is there almost for the taking. However it could easily take nine hours to collect, by hand, enough reed for a single square metre of roof!

Wheat straw is sometimes used for thatching for it is cheaper since it is the by product of a highly profitable farm crop which is harvested cheaply. Best quality thatching straw needs rather more gentle handling than the average 'combine' harvested crop, and will increasingly need to be grown as a specialist crop as the current trend in wheat breeding is for shorter straw length (with higher grain yield).

For small outhouses, the choice of high quality thatching material would be less vital; pratically anything from the fenland dyke has sufficed. In the New Forest the author once went 'rushcart' for the over winter thatch of the hay rick.

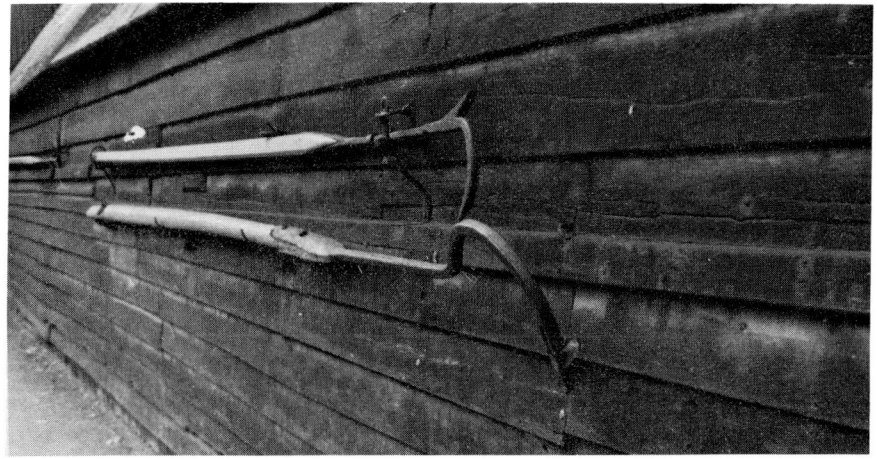

Fire hooks for tearing off burning thatch.

To protect against bird damage close mesh wire netting is used. Unfortunately the netting, which needs to be replaced frequently, adds to the fire hazard. This is because the most effective way to deal with a burning thatch roof is to tear it off as quickly as possible and netting impedes this action. Long poles with iron hooks were employed for this purpose and every thatch village had several at stragetic places and some still can be found.

Styles in thatching vary very interestingly over the whole country with locally developed patterns which have been handed down and maintained through the ages. In Suffolk the thatch rises to a slightly protruding point at the gable (Fig 9) and is fairly steeply pitched. In Norfolk and elsewhere the gable walls often rise above the level of the thatch. In parts of Essex, Cambridgeshire and West Suffolk there is another distinctive style (Fig 25 Map 6) with half hipped gable. In Suffolk, Norfolk, Cambridgeshire and Essex, elaborate shallow cut patterns may be found in the thatch. (Fig 30).

At one time fashion dictated that thatch was only the poor man's roofing and much was replaced by tiles, or even Welsh slate. It is recorded that one church had the thatch replaced by slate only on the side facing the road! This phase clearly passed before too much damage was done.

FIG 25 Half hipped thatched roof with tiny peak at ridge. This, together with the thatching of the dormer, are typical of many Essex and Cambridgeshire cottages.

A dormer with 'little more than a gentle lifting of the thatch'. Note horizontally opening windows (see Map 7, rear cover) (Wimblington, Cambs.).

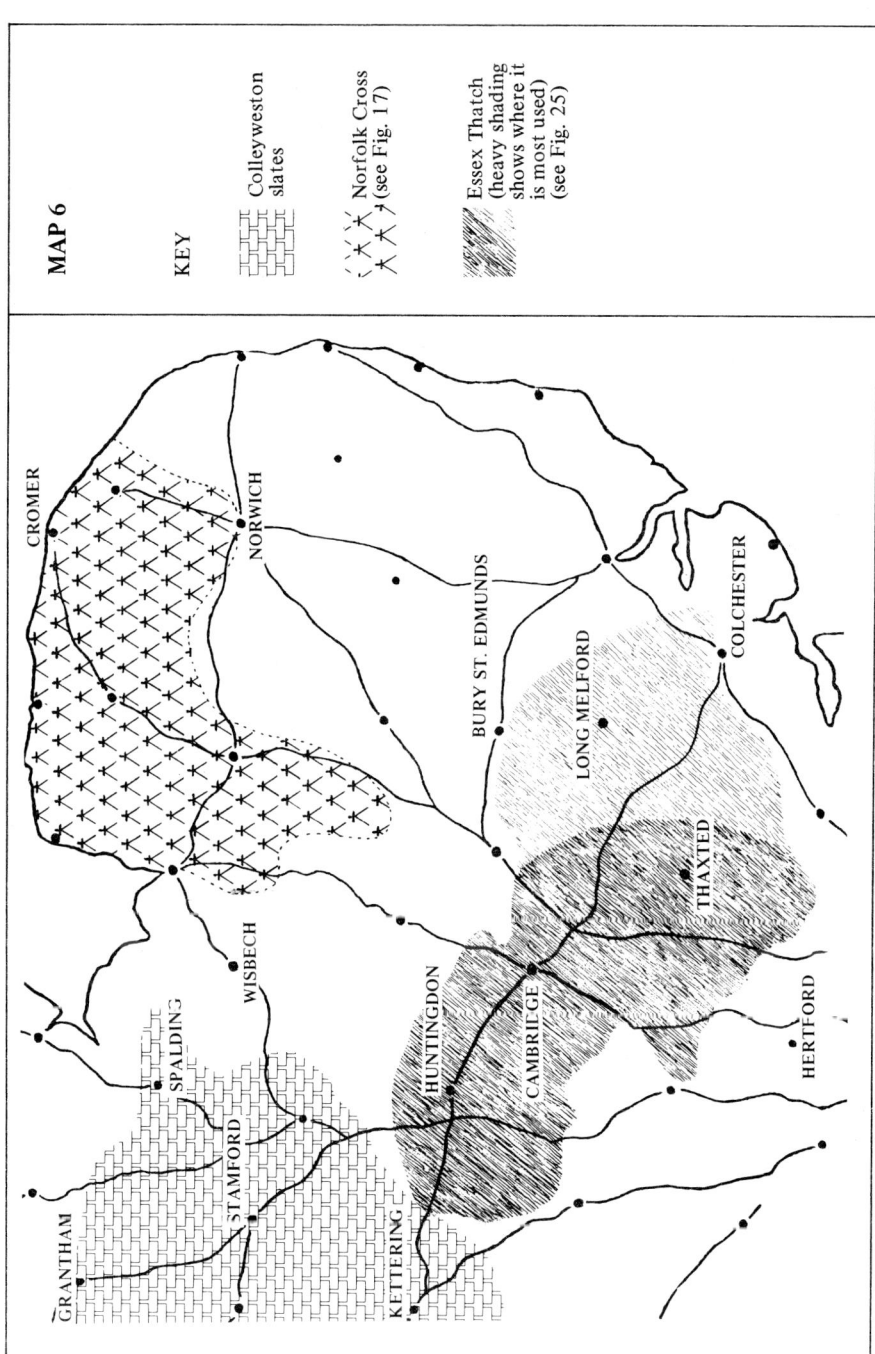

MAP 6

KEY

Colleyweston slates

Norfolk Cross (see Fig. 17)

Essex Thatch (heavy shading shows where it is most used) (see Fig. 25)

CROMER

NORWICH

BURY ST. EDMUNDS

COLCHESTER

LONG MELFORD

THAXTED

WISBECH

SPALDING

GRANTHAM

STAMFORD

KETTERING

HUNTINGDON

CAMBRIDGE

HERTFORD

COLLEYWESTON SLATE

The Collyweston slate makes a singular contribution to the beauty of the area. It was first employed in Roman times but fell out of use until the fourteenth century. The stone from which it is obtained occurs at the bottom of the limestone deposits and in a very limited area. It has quite the opposite characters of good building stone in that it readily fractures into thin, fairly smooth flat layers. In preparing the slates the stone slabs were quarried late in the year and kept as moist as possible so that the frost expansion of the water would achieve the splitting. Considerable hard work was then necessary to shape the stones and make a fixing hole. Production continues, on a limited scale, at a single quarry. (Map 6.)

A considerable renewing of roofs fortunately continues with the help of slates taken from outbuildings. Sadly 'synthetic' slates are now available which look very similar in shape and colour — only time will tell whether they remain as attractive as the real thing.

Obviously in the production processes the stone tends to break into very different sized pieces and the practice is — in common with **old** 'true' slates — to set the largest ones at the eaves and to work up to the ridge with smaller and smaller tiles. This economic necessity has added much to the beauty of this roofing material.

Near Collyweston itself all roofs down to those of the lowliest outhouse are of stone slates; the further one goes away from the area the grander must be the building if it is to have a stone roof. Away from the Collyweston area thatch and tiles increase steadily until only churches and Cambridge Colleges are found with stone slates.

Sunlight and shadow display the pleasing and characteristic texture of newly relaid Collyweston slates.

The cost of relaying slates is very high as each stone has to be given individual attention.

3   COTTAGE STYLES

Perhaps today we too readily strive to categorise anything and everything; we are obsessed by averages! But this simply may be an attempt to escape from, or at least cope with, the increasing complexities of modern life. Thus we seek to define the typical housewife, the typical corner shop, the typical three-bedroomed house. Then perhaps we may be excused for attempting to find the typical style of building for this area or for that. This proves quite a legitimate and reasonable thing to do in some places as certain areas really seem to have a style of their own.

FIG 26   Suffolk cottage of smallest possible size. Note wide splayed chimney with little outshut containing the oven.

The Suffolk Cottage

The tiny home depicted in Figure 26 combines very neatly all the main characters of a typical Suffolk dwelling. The window is exactly right (Fig 27), the walls are of lathe and plaster built on a red brick base which is often protected by a covering of tar. The thatch at the point of the gable protrudes slightly upwards and outwards. (see Fig 9). The chimney is particularly wide at the base (sometimes with an oven adjoining) and tapers very gradually until just a little below the ridge of the roof. (See Willy Lott's Cottage in 'The Haywain' by John Constable).

Such little cottage gems are rare but a very large proportion of the dwellings in Suffolk have most of these features convincingly enough to credit them as truly 'Suffolk Cottages'. Larger Suffolk dwelling houses tend to be tall in comparison with other areas.

In north east Suffolk flint is an important building material, near the coast red brick is more often employed.

FIG 27 The special Suffolk window.

The Suffolk Window

In the east and south of Suffolk there exists a type of window which has a particular appearance of lightness. This arises not only from its comparatively large size but from the manner in which the glass is set in the frame in T shaped glazing bars as shown in Figure 28. It will be seen that the glass pane, instead of being well recessed back into the frame, lies almost flush with its outer surface so giving a larger reflective area when viewed from outside.

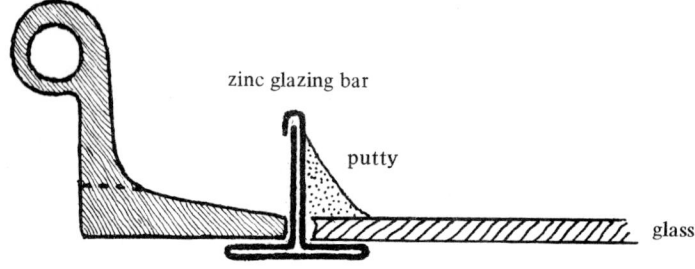

wrought iron frame and hinge

zinc glazing bar

putty

glass

FIG 28 Cross-section of Suffolk window.

Such framed windows can be found in many shapes and sizes, from single lights to five tall lights according to need and the means of the builder.

One type seems particularly characteristic of the area and is shown in Fig 27. In this the opening sash occupies the lower two thirds of the central light. These are not common but windows with this type of frame are readily found in the area indicated in Map 5.

FIG 29 Typical Fenland cottage, sloping to rear with wedge roofed dormer windows, chimneys in outside walls, red brick and red pantile roof.

Fenland Cottage

It seems that you either love the flat fenlands with their wide open skies and waving reeds or that you dislike them intensely. So fenland houses may either appear as the dullest utilitarian dwellings, or you may see something more in them with their pantiled roofs, redbrick walls, with chimneyed gable rising above the roof level, and sloping from two storeys in the front to one at the back, ('catslide'). The windows are small, fairly thick-framed and side-hinged; often there are wedge-shaped dormers. Occasionally there is a little decorative brickwork particularly just below the eaves.

Many Fenland cottages have had short lives due to the subsidence of the peat on which they have been built with inadequate foundations.

Norfolk Cottage

Not of a well-defined type but usually built of uncut ('unknapped') flint with red brick dressing. Occasionally red bricks reinforcing the walls, are laid in some degree of patterning. The roofs are generally of red pantiles but black pantiles are not uncommon. Many buildings are entirely of red brick with the gable wall some-times rising above roof level. Some ornamentation of brick work occasionally can be found.

FIG 30 Essex cottage with part of wall covered with weather boarding.

Cotswold Cottage

Much has already been written about the limestone buildings of the Stamford area. Apart from the wide display of fine stone masonry, the countryside of the area is particularly refreshing — partly because of the great amount of grassland! — but also in the landscape itself, so full of graceful spires and towers both on hills and in the valleys.

Essex Cottage

Thatch roof and plaster walls laid on brick footings are typical of Essex cottages (Fig 30, Map 6) with the thatch often half hipped in the manner detailed in Figure 25. The typical dormer is shown in Fig 9 on the left. Walls are often part or wholly weather board, plaster is often decorated with shallow patternings; exterior chimneys tend to be narrow down to the hearth level; windows tend to be small and their frames a little heavy. All these characters can be found elsewhere but seldom all together. In south Essex red flat tiles are particularly common and, in 'nearly modern' buildings, the yellow to grey 'London' brick, with its penny-sized black spots, is common.

Huntingdon Cottage

The main characters are the multicoloured tiles and bricks coupled with Mansard roof (Fig 10) with flat dormer windows which open by sliding sideways, central chimney — sometimes with plastered and pebble-dashed walls. Such houses can be found as far south as Cambridge. Its boundaries are set by the limestone to the north, the Fens to the east, the pink/reds of Bedfordshire and the Clunch and flint to south and south east. (Map 5).